Edwin Leigh

Gospel according to Saint John

Edited in Pronouncing Orthography

Edwin Leigh

Gospel according to Saint John
Edited in Pronouncing Orthography

ISBN/EAN: 9783337340513

Printed in Europe, USA, Canada, Australia, Japan

Cover: Foto ©Lupo / pixelio.de

More available books at **www.hansebooks.com**

THE GOSPEL

ACCORDING TO

SAINT J

EDITED IN

PRONOUNCING ORTH

BY

EDWIN LEI

———◦◦∘፨∘◦◦———

NEW YORK:
PRINTED FOR THE EDITOR.
1873.

PRONOUNCING ORTHOGRAPHY.

THIS print was first published in a pamphlet with this title.* For all practical purposes it will explain itself. Those who wish to know more about it, or about the methods and helps to learn and teach it, will please address EDWIN LEIGH, New York City.

A special form of a letter is used for each sound of it. The hair-line letters are silent. The pronunciation is according to our standard dictionaries, Webster and Worcester.

The 8 pairs of vowels, the diphthongs, and the semi-vowels (w y) are—

eel it, ale ell, air at, art ask ; urn up, or on, old folks, fool foot. ice oil our sue, use. we ye.

e i, a e, a a, a a; u u, o o, o o, o o. ioiouu, u. wy.

The aspirates, liquids, nasals, and the 8 pairs of consonants are—

hen when. lark. mining. veil if, the thin, is us, usual she, be up, do to, jet chin, go oat.

h wh. l r. m n ŋ. v f, th th, s s, s sh, b p, d t, j ch, g c.

To preserve the spelling, some duplicate forms are used. Notice their correspondence with the above forms for the same sounds.

police been women busy, they any bury, there, dove, all was beau sew, rude crew put.

i e o uy, a a u, e, o, a a, a w, u w u.

my boy now blew, ewe. quit one union. fur colonel r-r-roll. of laugh, discern size

y oy ow w, w. w v w. r r r. f h, q z

ice waltz, azure sure action ocean chaise, hiccough, iced, gem, kite quit lough exist ox.

c z, s s d c . ch, g, d, g, k q g, x x.

The old capitals are used like their small letters; the forms of the new ones generally correspond with the small letters for the same sounds. A few variations were found necessary, or desirable, but none of them are so great as some in the common alphabet; they are—

Aim	*Any,*	*Air,*	*Arm*	*Ask ;*	*Eight*	*Every.*	*Gem..*
Aa	Ae,	Aa,	Aa	Aa;	Ea	Ee.	Gg.

When the accent does not fall on the first syllable it is marked (').

---

* Entered according to Act of Congress, in the year 1864, by EDWIN LEIGH, in the Clerk's office of the U. S. District Court for the Eastern District of Missouri. Pat. May 19, 1868.

Entered according to Act of Congress, in the year 1873, by EDWIN LEIGH, in the office of the Librarian of Congress at Washington.

THE GOSPEL ACCORDING TO

ST. JOHN.

CHAPTER I.

1 In the begin'ning was the Word, and the Word was with God, and the Word was God.

2 The same was in the begin'ning with God.

3 All things were made by him; and without' him was not any thing made that was made.

4 In him was life; and the life was the light of men.

5 And the light shineth in darkness; and the darkness comprehend'ed it not.

6 ¶ There was a man sent from God, whose name was John.

7 The same came for a witness, to bear witness of the Light, that all men through him might believe'.

8 He was not that Light, but was sent to bear witness of that Light.

9 That was the true Light, which lighteth every man that cometh into the world.

10 He was in the world, and the world was made by him, and the world knew him not.

11 He came unto his own, and his own received' him not.

12 But as many as received' him, to them gave he power to become' the sons of God, even to them that believe' on his name:

13 Which were born, not of blood, nor of the will of the flesh, nor of the will of man, but of God.

14 And the Word was made flesh, and dwelt among' us, (and we beheld' his glory, the glory as of the only begot'ten of the Father,) full of grace and truth.

15 ¶ John bare witness of him, and cried, saying, This was he of whom I spake, He that cometh after me is preferred' before' me; for he was before' me.

16 And of his fulness have all we received', and grace for grace.

17 For the law was given by Moses, but grace and truth came by Jesus Christ.

18 No man hath seen God at any time; the only begot'ten Son, which is in the bosom of the Father, he hath declared' him.

19 ¶ And this is the record of John, when the Jews sent priests and Levites from Jeru'-salem to ask him, Who art thou?

20 And he confessed', and denied' not, but confessed', I am not the Christ.

21 And they asked him, What then? Art

thou Eli'as? And he saith, I am not. Art thou that Prophet? And he answered, No.

22 Then said they unto him, Who art thou? that we may give an answer to them that sent us. What sayest thou of thyself?

23 He said, I am the voice of one crying in the wilderness, Make straight the way of the Lord, as said the prophet Esa'ias.

24 And they which were sent were of the Pharisees.

25 And they asked him, and said unto him, Why baptiz'est thou then, if thou be not that Christ, nor Eli'as, neither that Prophet?

26 John answered them, saying, I baptize' with water: but there standeth one among' you, whom ye know not;

27 He it is, who coming after me is preferred' before' me, whose shoe's latchet I am not worthy to unloose'.

28 These things were done in Bethab'ara beyond' Jordan, where John was baptiz'ing.

29 ¶ The next day, John seeth Jesus coming unto him, and saith, Behold' the Lamb of God, which taketh away' the sin of the world!

30 This is he of whom I said, After me cometh a man which is preferred' before' me; for he was before' me.

31 And I knew him not: but that he should be made manifest to Israel, therefore am I come baptiz'ing with water.

32 And John bare record, saying, I saw the

Spirit descend'ing from heaven like a dove, and it abode' upon' him.

33 And I knew him not: but he that sent me to baptize' with water, the same said unto me, Upon' whom thou shalt see the Spirit descend'ing, and remain'ing on him, the same is he which baptiz'eth with the Holy Ghost.

34 And I saw, and bare record that this is the Son of God.

35 ¶ Again' the next day after, John stood, and two of his disci'ples;

36 And looking upon' Jesus as he walked, he saith, Behold' the Lamb of God!

37 And the two disci'ples heard him speak, and they followed Jesus.

38 Then Jesus turned, and saw them following, and saith unto them, What seek ye? They said unto him, Rabbi, (which is to say, being inter'preted, Master,) where dwellest thou?

39 He saith unto them, Come and see. They came and saw where he dwelt, and abode' with him that day: for it was about' the tenth hour.

40 One of the two which heard John speak, and followed him, was Andrew, Simon Peter's brother.

41 He first findeth his own brother Simon, and saith unto him, We have found the Messi'as, which is, being inter'preted, the Christ.

42 And he brought him to Jesus. And

when Jesus beheld' him, he said, Thou art Simon the son of Jona: thou shalt be called Cepfias, which is by inter'preta'tion, A stone.

43 ¶ The day following Jesus would go forth into Galilee, and findeth Pfilip, and saith unto him, Follow me.

44 Now Pfilip was of Bethsa'ida, the city of Andrew and Peter.

45 Pfilip findeth Nathan'ael, and saith unto him, We have found him, of whom Moses in the law, and the propfiets, did write, Jesus of Nazareth, the son of Josepfi.

46 And Nathan'ael said unto him, Can there any good thing come out of Nazareth? Pfilip saith unto him, Come and see.

47 Jesus saw Nathan'ael coming to him, and saith of him, Behold' an Israelite indeed', in whom is no guile!

48 Nathan'ael saith unto him, Whence knowest thou me? Jesus answered and said unto him, Before' that Pfilip called thee, when thou wast under the fig tree, I saw thee.

49 Nathan'ael answered and saith unto him, Rabbi, thou art the Son of God; thou art the King of Israel.

50 Jesus answered and said unto him, Because' I said unto thee, I saw thee under the fig tree, believ'est thou? thou shalt see greater things than these.

51 And he saith unto him, Verily, verily, I say unto you, Hereaft'er ye shall see heaven

open, and the angels of God ascend'ing and descend'ing upon' the Son of man.

CHAPTER II.

1 And the third day there was a marriage in Cana of Galilee; and the mother of Jesus was there:

2 And both Jesus was called, and his disci'-ples, to the marriage.

3 And when they wanted wine, the mother of Jesus saith unto him, They have no wine.

4 Jesus saith unto her, Woman, what have I to do with thee? mine hour is not yet come.

5 His mother saith unto the servants, What-soev'er he saith unto you, do it.

6 And there were set there six waterpots of stone, after the manner of the purifying of the Jews, contain'ing two or three firkins apiece'.

7 Jesus saith unto them, Fill the water-pots with water. And they filled them up to the brim.

8 And he saith unto them, Draw out now, and bear unto the governor of the feast. And they bare it.

9 When the ruler of the feast had tasted the water that was made wine, and knew not whence it was, (but the servants which drew the water knew,) the governor of the feast called the bridegroom,

10 And saith unto him, Every man at the

begin'ning doth set forth good wine; and when men have well drunk, then that which is worse: but thou hast kept the good wine until' now. .

11 This begin'ning of miracles did Jesus in Cana of Galilee, and manifested forth his glory; and his disci'ples believed' on him.

12 ¶ After this he went down to Caper'na-um, he, and his mother, and his brethren, and his disci'ples; and they contin'ued there not many days.

13 ¶ And the Jews' passover was at hand, and Jesus went up to Jeru'salem,

14 And found in the temple those that sold oxen and sheep and doves, and the changers of money sitting:

15 And when he had made a scourge of small cords, he drove them all out of the temple, and the sheep, and the oxen; and poured out the changers' money, and over-threw' the tables;

16 And said unto them that sold doves, Take these things hence; make not my Fa-ther's house a house of merchandise.

17 And his disci'ples remem'bered that it was written, The zeal of thine house hath eaten me up.

18 ¶ Then answered the Jews and said un-to him, What sign shewest thou unto us, see-ing that thou doest these things?

19 Jesus answered and said unto them, De-

stroy' this temple, and in three days I will raise it up.

20 Then said the Jews, Forty and six years was this temple in building, and wilt thou rear it up in three days?

21 But he spake of the temple of his body.

22 When therefore he was risen from the dead, his disci'ples remem'bered that he had said this unto them; and they believed' the Scripture, and the word which Jesus had said.

23 ¶ Now when he was in Jeru'salem at the passover, in the feast day, many believed' in his name, when they saw the miracles which he did.

24 But Jesus did not commit' himself' unto them, because' he knew all men,

25 And needed not that any should testify of man; for he knew what was in man.

CHAPTER III.

1 There was a man of the Pharisees, named Nicode'mus, a ruler of the Jews:

2 The same came to Jesus by night, and said unto him, Rabbi, we know that thou art a teacher come from God: for no man can do these miracles that thou doest, except'. God be with him.

3 Jesus answered and said unto him, Verily, verily, I say unto thee, Except' a man be born again', he cannot see the kingdom of God.

4 Nicode'mus saith unto him, How can a man be born when he is old? can he enter the second time into his mother's womb, and be born?

5 Jesus answered, Verily, verily, I say unto thee, Except' a man be born of water and of the Spirit, he cannot enter into the kingdom of God.

6 That which is born of the flesh is flesh; and that which is born of the Spirit is spirit.

7 Marvel not that I said unto thee, Ye must be born again'.

8 The wind bloweth where it listeth, and thou hearest the sound thereof', but canst not tell whence it cometh, and whither it goeth: so is every one that is born of the Spirit.

9 Nicode'mus answered and said unto him, How can these things be?

10 Jesus answered and said unto him, Art thou a master of Israel, and knowest not these things?

11 Verily, verily, I say unto thee, We speak that we do know, and testify that we have seen; and ye receive' not our witness.

12 If I have told you earthly things, and ye believe' not, how shall ye believe', if I tell you of heavenly things?

13 And no man hath ascend'ed up to heaven, but he that came down from heaven, even the Son of man which is in heaven.

14 ¶ And as Moses lifted up the serpent in the wilderness, even so must the Son of man be lifted up:

15 That whosoev'er believ'eth in him should not perish, but have eter'nal life.

16 ¶ For God so loved the world, that he gave his only begot'ten Son, that whosoev'er believ'eth in him should not perish, but have everlast'ing life.

17 For God sent not his Son into the world to condemn' the world; but that the world through him might be saved.

18 ¶ He that believ'eth on him is not condemned': but he that believ'eth not is condemned' alread'y, because' he hath not believed' in the name of the only begot'ten Son of God.

19 And this is the condemna'tion, that light is come into the world, and men loved darkness rather than light, because' their deeds were evil.

20 For every one that doeth evil hateth the light, neither cometh to the light, lest his deeds should be reproved'.

21 But he that doeth truth cometh to the light, that his deeds may be made manifest, that they are wrought in God.

22 ¶ After these things came Jesus and his disci'ples into the land of Jude'a; and there he tarried with them, and baptized'.

23 ¶ And John also was baptiz'ing in Enon

near to Salim, because' there was much water thare: and thay came, and were baptized'.

24 For John was not yet cast into prison.

25 ¶ Then thare arose' a question between' some of John's disci'ples and the Jews about' purifying.

26 And thay came unto John, and said unto him, Rabbi, he that was with thee beyond' Jordan, to whom thou barest witness, behold', the same baptiz'eth, and all men come to him.

27 John answered and said, A man can receive' nothing, except' it be given him from heaven.

28 Ye yourselves' bear me witness, that I said, I am not the Christ, but that I am sent before' him.

29 He that hath the bride is the bridegroom: but the friend of the bridegroom, which standeth and heareth him, rejoic'eth greatly because' of the bridegroom's voice: this my joy therefore is fulfilled'.

30 He must increase', but I must decrease'.

31 He that cometh from above' is above' all: he that is of the earth is earthly, and speaketh of the earth: he that cometh from heaven is above' all.

32 And what he hath seen and heard, that he testifieth; and no man receiv'eth his testimony.

33 He that hath received' his testimony hath set to his seal that God is true.

34 For he whom God hath sent speaketh the words of God: for God giveth not the Spirit by measure unto him.

35 The Father loveth the Son, and hath given all things into his hand.

36 He that believ'eth on the Son hath ever-last'ing life: and he that believ'eth not the Son shall not see life; but the wrath of God abid'eth on him.

CHAPTER IV.

1 When therefore the Lord knew how the Pharisees had heard that Jesus made and bap-tized' more disci'ples than John,

2 (Though Jesus himself' baptized' not, but his disci'ples,)

3 He left Jude'a, and depart'ed again' into Galilee.

4 And he must needs go through Sama'ria.

5 Then cometh he to a city of Sama'ria, which is called Sychar, near to the parcel of ground that Jacob gave to his son Joseph.

6 Now Jacob's well was there. Jesus there-fore, being wearied with his journey, sat thus on the well: and it was about' the sixth hour.

7 There cometh a woman of Sama'ria to draw water: Jesus saith unto her, Give me to drink.

8 (For his disci'ples were gone away' unto the city to buy meat.)

9 Then saith the woman of Sama'ria unto him, How is it that thou, being a Jew, askest

driŋk of me, which am a woman of Sama'ria? for the Jews have no dealiŋgs with the Samar'itans.

10 Jesus answered and said unto her, If thou knewest the gift of God, and who it is that saith to thee, Give me to driŋk; thou wouldst have asked of him, and he would have given thee liviŋg water.

11 The woman saith unto him, Sir, thou hast nothiŋg to draw with, and the well is deep: from whence then hast thou that liviŋg water?

12 Art thou greater than our father Jacob, which gave us the well, and draŋk thereof' himself', and his children, and his cattle?

13 Jesus answered and said unto her, Whosoev'er driŋketh of this water shall thirst again':

14 But whosoev'er driŋketh of the water that I shall give him shall never thirst; but the water that I shall give him shall be in him a well of water spriŋgiŋg up into everlast'iŋg life.

15 The woman saith unto him, Sir, give me this water, that I thirst not, neither come hither to draw.

16 Jesus saith unto her, Go, call thy husband, and come hither.

17 The woman answered and said, I have no husband. Jesus said unto her, Thou hast well said, I have no husband:

18 For thou hast had five husbands; and he

whom thou now hast is not thy husband: in that saidst thou truly.

19 The woman saith unto him, Sir, I perceive' that thou art a prophet.

20 Our fathers worshiped in this mountain; and ye say, that in Jeru'salem is the place where men ought to worship.

21 Jesus saith unto her, Woman, believe' me, the hour cometh, when ye shall neither in this mountain, nor yet at Jeru'salem, worship the Father.

22 Ye worship ye know not what: we know what we worship; for salva'tion is of the Jews.

23 But the hour cometh, and now is, when the true worshipers shall worship the Father in spirit and in truth: for the Father seeketh such to worship him.

24 God is a Spirit: and they that worship him must worship him in spirit and in truth.

25 The woman saith unto him, I know that Messi'as cometh which is called Christ: when he is come, he will tell us all things.

26 Jesus saith unto her, I that speak unto thee am he.

27 ¶ And upon' this came his disci'ples, and marveled that he talked with the woman: yet no man said, What seekest thou? or, Why talkest thou with her?

28 The woman then left her waterpot, and went her way into the city, and saith to the men,

29 Come, see a man, which told me all things that ever I did: is not this the Christ?

30 Then they went out of the city, and came unto him.

31 ¶ In the mean while his disci'ples prayed him, saying, Master, eat.

32 But he said unto them, I have meat to eat that ye know not of.

33 Therefore said the disci'ples one to an-oth'er, Hath any man brought him aught to eat?

34 Jesus saith unto them, My meat is to do the will of him that sent me, and to finish his work.

35 Say not ye, There are yet four months, and then cometh harvest? behold', I say unto you, Lift up your eyes, and look on the fields; for they are white alread'y to harvest.

36 And he that reapeth receiv'eth wages, and gathereth fruit unto life eter'nal: that both he that soweth and he that reapeth may rejoice' togeth'er.

37 And herein' is that saying true, One sow-eth, and anoth'er reapeth.

38 I sent you to reap that whereon' ye be-stowed' no labor: other men labored, and ye are entered into their labors.

39 ¶ And many of the Samar'itans of that city believed' on him for the saying of the woman, which testified, He told me all that ever I did.

40 So when the Samar'itans were come unto him, they besought' him that he would tarry with them: and he abode' there two days.

41 And many more believed' because' of his own word;

42 And said unto the woman, Now we believe', not because' of thy saying: for we have heard him ourselves', and know that this is indeed' the Christ, the Savior of the world.

43 ¶ Now after two days he depart'ed thence, and went into Galilee.

44 For Jesus himself' testified, that a propfiet hath no honor in his own country.

45 Then when he was come into Galilee, the Galile'ans received' him, having seen all the things that he did at Jeru'salem at the feast: for they also went unto the feast.

46 So Jesus came again' into Cana of Galilee, where he made the water wine. And there was a certain nobleman, whose son was sick at Caper'naum.

47 When he heard that Jesus was come out of Jude'a into Galilee, he went unto him, and besought' him that he would come down, and heal his son: for he was at the point of death.

48 Then said Jesus unto him, Except' ye see signs and wonders, ye will not believe'.

49 The nobleman saith unto him, Sir, come down are my child die.

50 Jesus saith unto him, Go thy way; thy son liveth. And the man believed' the word

that Jesus had spoken unto him, and he went his way.

51 And as he was now going down, his servants met him, and told him, saying, Thy son liveth.

52 Then inquired' he of them the hour when he began' to amend'. And they said unto him, Yesterday at the seventh hour the fever left him.

53 So the father knew that it was at the same hour, in the which Jesus said unto him, Thy son liveth: and himself' believed', and his whole house.

54 This is again' the second miracle that Jesus did, when he was come out of Jude'a into Galilee.

CHAPTER V.

1 After this there was a feast of the Jews; and Jesus went up to Jeru'salem.

2 Now there is at Jeru'salem by the sheep market a pool, which is called in the Hebrew tongue Bethes'da, having five porches.

3 In these lay a great multitude of impotent folk, of blind, halt, withered, waiting for the moving of the water.

4 For an angel went down at a certain season into the pool, and troubled the water: whosoev'er then first after the troubling of the water stepped in was made whole of whatsoev'er disease' he had.

5 And a certain man was there, which had an infirm'ity thirty and eight years.

6 When Jesus saw him lie, and knew that he had been now a long time in that case, he saith unto him, Wilt thou be made whole?

7 The impotent man answered him, Sir, I have no man, when the water is troubled, to put me into the pool: but while I am coming, anoth'er steppeth down before' me.

8 Jesus saith unto him, Rise, take up thy bed, and walk.

9 And imme'diately the man was made whole, and took up his bed, and walked: and on the same day was the sabbath.

10 ¶ The Jews therefore said unto him that was cured, It is the sabbath day: it is not lawful for thee to carry thy bed.

11 He answered them, He that made me whole, the same said unto me, Take up thy bed, and walk.

12 Then asked they him, What man is that which said unto thee, Take up thy bed, and walk?

13 And he that was healed wist not who it was: for Jesus had conveyed' himself' away', a multitude being in that place.

14 Afterward Jesus findeth him in the temple, and said unto him, Behold', thou art made whole: sin no more, lest a worse thing come unto thee.

15 The man depart'ed, and told the Jews

that it was Jesus, which had made him whole.

16 And therefore did the Jews persecute Jesus, and sought to slay him, because' he had done these things on the sabbath day.

17 ¶ But Jesus answered them, My Father worketh hitherto', and I work.

18 Therefore the Jews sought the more to kill him, because' he not only had broken the sabbath, but said also that God was his Father, making himself' equal with God.

19 Then answered Jesus and said unto them, Verily, verily, I say unto you, The Son can do nothing of himself', but what he seeth the Father do: for what things soev'er he doeth, these also doeth the Son likewise.

20 For the Father loveth the Son, and sheweth him all things that himself' doeth: and he will shew him greater works than these, that ye may marvel.

21 For as the Father raiseth up the dead, and quickeneth them; even so the Son quickeneth whom he will.

22 For the Father judgeth no man, but hath commit'ted all judgment unto the Son:

23 That all men should honor the Son, even as they honor the Father. He that honoreth not the Son honoreth not the Father which hath sent him.

24 Verily, verily, I say unto you, He that heareth my word, and believ'eth on him that

sent me, hath everlast'ing life, and shall not come into condemna'tion; but is passed from death unto life.

25 Verily, verily, I say unto you, The hour is coming, and now is, when the dead shall hear the voice of the Son of God: and they that hear shall live.

26 For as the Father hath life in himself'; so hath he given to the Son to have life in him-self';

27 And hath given him author'ity to execute judgment also, because' he is the Son of man.

28 Marvel not at this: for the hour is coming, in the which all that are in the graves shall hear his voice,

29 And shall come forth; they that have done good, unto the resurrec'tion of life; and they that have done evil, unto the resurrec'-tion of damna'tion.

30 I can of mine own self do nothing: as I hear, I judge: and my judgment is just; be-cause' I seek not mine own will, but the will of the Father which hath sent me.

31 If I bear witness of myself', my witness is not true.

32 ¶ There is anoth'er that beareth witness of me: and I know that the witness which he witnesseth of me is true.

33 Ye sent unto John, and he bare witness unto the truth.

34 But I receive' not testimony from man:

but these things I say, that ye might be saved.

35 He was a burning and a shining light: and ye were willing for a season to rejoice′ in his light.

36 ¶ But I have greater witness than that of John: for the works which the Father hath given me to finish, the same works that I do, bear witness of me, that the Father hath sent me.

37 And the Father himself′, which hath sent me, hath borne witness of me. Ye have neither heard his voice at any time, nor seen his shape.

38 And ye have not his word abid′ing in you: for whom he hath sent, him ye believe′ not.

39 ¶ Search the Scriptures; for in them ye think ye have eter′nal life: and they are they which testify of me.

40 And ye will not come to me, that ye might have life.

41 I receive′ not honor from men.

42 But I know you, that ye have not the love of God in you.

43 I am come in my Father's name, and ye receive′ me not: if anoth′er shall come in his own name, him ye will receive′.

44 How can ye believe′, which receive′ honor one of anoth′er, and seek not the honor that cometh from God only?

45 Do not think that I will accuse′ you to

the Father: there is one that accus'eth you, even Moses, in whom ye trust.

46 For had ye believed' Moses, ye would have believed' me: for he wrote of me.

47 But if ye believe' not his writings, how shall ye believe' my words?

CHAPTER VI.

1 After these things Jesus went over the sea of Galilee, which is the sea of Tibe'rias.

2 And a great multitude followed him, because' they saw his miracles which he did on them that were diseased'.

3 And Jesus went up into a mountain, and there he sat with his disci'ples.

4 And the passover, a feast of the Jews, was nigh.

5 ¶ When Jesus then lifted up his eyes, and saw a great company come unto him, he saith unto Philip, Whence shall we buy bread, that these may eat?

6 And this he said to prove him: for he himself' knew what he would do.

7 Philip answered him, Two hundred pennyworth of bread is not suffi'cient for them, that every one of them may take a little.

8 One of his disci'ples, Andrew, Simon Peter's brother, saith unto him,

9 There is a lad here, which hath five barley loaves, and two small fishes: but what are they among' so many?

10 And Jesus said, Make the men sit down. Now there was much grass in the place. So the men sat down, in number about' five thousand.

11 And Jesus took the loaves; and when he had given thanks, he distrib'uted to the disci'ples, and the disci'ples to them that were set down; and likewise of the fishes as much as they would.

12 When they were filled, he said unto his disci'ples, Gather up the fragments that remain', that nothing be lost.

13 Therefore they gathered them togeth'er, and filled twelve baskets with the fragments of the five barley loaves, which remained' over and above' unto them that had eaten.

14 Then those men, when they had seen the miracle that Jesus did, said, This is of a truth that Prophet that should come into the world.

15 ¶ When Jesus therefore perceived' that they would come and take him by force, to make him a king, he depart'ed again' into a mountain himself' alone'.

16 And when even was now come, his disci'ples went down unto the sea,

17 And entered into a ship, and went over the sea toward Caper'naum. And it was now dark, and Jesus was not come to them.

18 And the sea arose' by reason of a great wind that blew.

19 So when they had rowed about' five and

twenty or thirty furlongs, they see Jesus walk-
ing on the sea, and drawing nigh unto the
ship: and they were afraid'.

20 But he saith unto them, It is I; be not
afraid'.

21 Then they willingly received' him into
the ship: and imme'diately the ship was at
the land whither they went.

22 ¶ The day following, when the people,
which stood on the other side of the sea, saw
that there was none other boat there, save
that one whereinto' his disci'ples were entered,
and that Jesus went not with his disci'ples into the boat, but that his disci'ples were gone
away' alone';

23 Howbe'it there came other boats from Tibe'rias nigh unto the place where they did eat
bread, after that the Lord had given thanks:

24 When the people therefore saw that Jesus was not there, neither his disci'ples, they
also took shipping, and came to Caper'naum,
seeking for Jesus.

25 And when they had found him on the
other side of the sea, they said unto him,
Rabbi, when camest thou hither?

26 Jesus answered them and said, Verily,
verily, I say unto you, Ye seek me, not because' ye saw the miracles, but because' ye
did eat of the loaves, and were filled.

27 Labor not for the meat which perisheth,
but for that meat which endur'eth unto ever-

last'ing life, which the Son of man shall give unto you: for him hath God the Father sealed.

28 Then said they unto him, What shall we do, that we might work the works of God?

29 Jesus answered and said unto them, This is the work of God, that ye believe' on him whom he hath sent.

30 They said therefore unto him, What sign shewest thou then, that we may see, and believe' thee? what dost thou work?

31 Our fathers did eat manna in the desert; as it is written, He gave them bread from heaven to eat.

32 Then Jesus said unto them, Verily, verily, I. say unto you, Moses gave you not that bread from heaven; but my Father giveth you the true bread from heaven.

33 For the bread of God is he which cometh down from heaven, and giveth life unto the world.

34 Then said they unto him, Lord, evermore' give us this bread.

35 And Jesus said unto them, I am the bread of life; he that cometh to me shall never hunger; and he that believ'eth on me shall never thirst.

36 But I said unto you, That ye also have seen me, and believe' not.

37 All that the Father giveth me shall come to me; and him that cometh to me I will in no wise cast out.

38 For I came down from heaven, not to do mine own will, but the will of him that sent me.

39 And this is the Father's will which hath sent me, that of all which he hath given me I should lose nothing, but should raise it up again' at the last day.

40 And this is the will of him that sent me, that every one which seeth the Son, and believ'eth on him, may have everlast'ing life: and I will raise him up at the last day.

41 The Jews then murmured at him, because' he said, I am the bread which came down from heaven.

42 And they said, Is not this Jesus, the son of Joseph, whose father and mother we know? how is it then that he saith, I came down from heaven?

43 Jesus therefore answered and said unto them, Murmur not among' yourselves'.

44 No man can come to me, except' the Father which hath sent me draw him: and I will raise him up at the last day.

45 It is written in the propfiets, And they shall be all taught of God. Every man therefore that hath heard, and hath learned of the Father, cometh unto me.

46 Not that any man hath seen the Father, save he which is of God, he hath seen the Father.

47 Verily, verily, I say unto you, He that believ'eth on me hath everlast'ing life.

48 I am that bread of life.

49 Your fathers did eat manna in the wilderness, and are dead.

50 This is the bread which cometh down from heaven, that a man may eat thereof', and not die.

51 I, am the living bread which came down from heaven: if any man eat of this bread, he shall live for ever: and the bread that I will give is my flesh, which I will give for the life of the world.

52 The Jews therefore strove among' themselves', saying, How can this man give us his flesh to eat?

53 Then Jesus said unto them, Verily, verily, I say unto you, Except' ye eat the flesh of the Son of man, and drink his blood, ye have no life in you.

54 Whoso eateth my flesh, and drinketh my blood, hath eter'nal life; and I will raise him up at the last day.

55 For my flesh is meat indeed', and my blood is drink indeed'.

56 He that eateth my flesh, and drinketh my blood, dwelleth in me, and I in him.

57 As the living Father hath sent me, and I live by the Father; so he that eateth me, even he shall live by me.

58 This is that bread which came down from heaven: not as your fathers did eat manna, and are dead: he that eateth of this bread shall live for ever.

59 These things said he in the synagogue, as he taught in Caper'naum.

60 Many therefore of his disci'ples, when they had heard this, said, This is a hard saying; who can hear it?

61 When Jesus knew in himself' that his disci'ples murmured at it he said unto them, Doth this offend' you?

62 What and if ye shall see the Son of man ascend' up where he was before'?

63 It is the Spirit that quickeneth; the flesh profiteth nothing: the words that I speak unto you, thay are spirit, and thay are life.

64 But thare are some of you that believe' not. For Jesus knew from the begin'ning who thay were that believed' not, and who should betray' him.

65 And he said, Therefore said I unto you, that no man can come unto me, except' it were given unto him of my Father.

66 ¶ From that time many of his disci'ples went back, and walked no more with him.

67 Then said Jesus unto the twelve, Will ye also go away'?

68 Then Simon Peter answered him, Lord, to whom shall we go? thou hast the words of eter'nal life.

69 And we believe' and are sure that thou art that Christ, the Son of the living God.

70 Jesus answered them, Have not I chosen you twelve, and one of you is a devil?

71 He spake of Judas Iscar'iot the son of Simon: for he it was that should betray' him, being one of the twelve.

CHAPTER VII.

1 After these things Jesus walked in Galilee: for he would not walk in Jewry, because' the Jews sought to kill him.

2 Now the Jews' feast of tabernacles was at hand.

3 His brethren therefore said unto him, Depart' hence, and go into Jude'a, that thy disci'ples also may see the works that thou doest.

4 For there is no man that doeth any thing in secret, and he himself' seeketh to be known openly. If thou do these things, shew thyself' to the world.

5 For neither did his brethren believe' in him.

6 Then Jesus said unto them, My time is not yet come: but your time is always ready.

7 The world cannot hate you; but me it hateth, because' I testify of it, that the works thereof' are evil.

8 Go ye up unto this feast: I go not up yet unto this feast; for my time is not yet full come.

9 When he had said these words unto them, he abode' still in Galilee.

10 ¶ But when his brethren were gone up,

then went he also up unto the feast, not openly, but as it were in secret.

11 Then the Jews sought him at the feast, and said, Where is he?

12 And there was much murmuring among the people concern'ing him: for some said, He is a good man: others said, Nay; but he deceiv'eth the people.

13 Howbe'it no man spake openly of him for fear of the Jews.

14 ¶ Now about' the midst of the feast Jesus went up into the temple, and taught.

15 And the Jews marveled, saying, How knoweth this man letters, having never· learned?

16 Jesus answered them, and said, My doctrine is not mine, but his that sent me.

17 If any man will do his will, he shall know of the doctrine, whether it be of God, or whether I speak of myself'.

18 He that speaketh of himself' seeketh his own glory: but he that seeketh his glory that sent him, the same is true, and no unright'eousness is in him.

19 Did not Moses give you the law, and yet none of you keepeth the law? Why go ye about' to kill me?

20 The people answered and said, Thou hast a devil: who goeth about' to kill thee?

21 Jesus answered and said unto them, I have done one work, and ye all marvel.

22 Moses therefore gave unto you circumcis'-

ion; (not because' it is of Moses, but of the fathers;) and ye on the sabbath day circumcise a man.

23 If a man on the sabbath day receive' circumcis'ion, that the law of Moses should not be broken; are ye angry at me, because' I have made a man every whit whole on the sabbath day?

24 Judge not accord'ing to the appear'ance, but judge righteous judgment.

25 Then said some of them of Jeru'salem, Is not this he, whom they seek to kill?

26 But, lo, he speaketh boldly, and they say nothing unto him. Do the rulers know indeed' that this is the very Christ?

27 Howbe'it we know this man whence he is: but when Christ cometh, no man knoweth whence he is.

28 Then cried Jesus in the temple as he taught, saying, Ye both know me, and ye know whence I am: and I am not come of myself', but he that sent me is true, whom ye know not.

29 But I know him; for I am from him, and he hath sent me.

30 Then they sought to take him: but no man laid hands on him, because' his hour was not yet come.

31 And many of the people believed' on him, and said, When Christ cometh, will he do more miracles than these which this man hath done?

32 ¶ The Pharisees heard that the people murmured such things concern'ing him; and the Pharisees and the chief priests sent officers to take him.

33 Then said Jesus unto them, Yet a little while am I with you, and then I go unto him that sent me.

34 Ye shall seek me, and shall not find me: and where I am, thither ye cannot come.

35 Then said the Jews among' themselves', Whither will he go, that we shall not find him? will he go unto the dispersed' among' the Gentiles, and teach the Gentiles?

36 What manner of saying is this that he said, Ye shall seek me, and shall not find me: and where I am, thither ye cannot come?

37 In the last day, that great day of the feast, Jesus stood and cried, saying, If any man thirst, let him come unto me, and drink.

38 He that believ'eth on me, as the Scripture hath said, out of his belly shall flow rivers of living water.

39 (But this spake he of the Spirit, which they that believe' on him should receive': for the Holy Ghost was not yet given; because' that Jesus was not yet glorified.)

40 ¶ Many of the people therefore, when they heard this saying, said, Of a truth this is the Prophet.

41 Others said, This is the Christ. But some said, Shall Christ come out of Galilee?

42 Hath not the Scripture said, That Christ cometh of the seed of David, and out of the town of Bethlehem, where David was?

43 So there was a divis'ion among' the people because' of him.

44 And some of them would have taken him; but no man laid hands on him.

45 ¶ Then came the officers to the chief priests and Pharisees; and they said unto them, Why have ye not brought him?

46 The officers answered, Never man spake like this man.

47 Then answered them the Pharisees, Are ye also deceived'?

48 Have any of the rulers or of the Pharisees believed' on him?

49 But this people who knoweth not the law are cursed.

50 Nicode'mus saith unto them, (he that came to Jesus by night, being one of them,)

51 Doth our law judge any man, before' it hear him, and know what he doeth?

52 They answered and said unto him, Art thou also of Galilee? Search, and look: for out of Galilee aris'eth no prophet.

53 And every man went unto his own house.

CHAPTER VIII.

1 Jesus went unto the mount of Olives.

2 And early in the morning he came again'

into the temple, and all the people came unto him; and he sat down, and taught them.

3 And the scribes and Pharisees brought unto him a woman taken in adul'tery; and when they had set her in the midst,

4 They say unto him, Master, this woman was taken in adul'tery, in the very act.

5 Now Moses in the law command'ed us, that such should be stoned: but what sayest thou?

6 This they said, tempting him, that they might have to accuse' him. But Jesus stooped down, and with his finger wrote on the ground, as though he heard them not.

7 So when they contin'ued asking him, he lifted up himself', and said unto them, He that is without' sin among' you, let him first cast a stone at her.

8 And again' he stooped down, and wrote on the ground.

9 And they which heard it, being convict'ed by their own conscience, went out one by one, begin'ning at the eldest, even unto the last: and Jesus was left alone', and the woman standing in the midst.

10 When Jesus had lifted up himself', and saw none but the woman, he said unto her, Woman, where are those thine accus'ers? hath no man condemned' thee?

11 She said, No man, Lord. And Jesus said

unto her, Neither do I condemn' thee: go, and sin no more.

12 ¶ Then spake Jesus again' unto them, saying, I am the light of the world: he that followeth me shall not walk in darkness, but shall have the light of life.

13 The Pharisees therefore said unto him, Thou bearest record of thyself'; thy record is not true.

14 Jesus answered and said unto them, Though I bear record of myself', yet my record is true: for I know whence I came, and whither I go; but ye cannot tell whence I come, and whither I go.

15 Ye judge after the flesh; I judge no man.

16 And yet if I judge, my judgment is true: for I am not alone', but I and the Father that sent me.

17 It is also written in your law, that the testimony of two men is true.

18 I am one that bear witness of myself', and the Father that sent me beareth witness of me.

19 Then said they unto him, Where is thy Father? Jesus answered, Ye neither know me, nor my Father: if ye had known me, ye should have known my Father also.

20 These words spake Jesus in the treasury, as he taught in the temple: and no man laid hands on him; for his hour was not yet come.

21 Then said Jesus again' unto them, I go

my way, and ye shall seek me, and shall die in your sins: whither I go, ye cannot come.

22 Then said the Jews, Will he kill himself? because' he saith, Whither I go, ye cannot come.

23 And he said unto them, Ye are from beneath'; I am from above': ye are of this world; I am not of this world.

24 I said therefore unto you, that ye shall die in your sins: for if ye believe' not that I am he, ye shall die in your sins.

25 Then said they unto him, Who art thou? And Jesus saith unto them, Even the same that I said unto you from the begin'ning.

26 I have many things to say and to judge of you: but he that sent me is true; and I speak to the world those things which I have heard of him.

27 They understood' not that he spake to them of the Father.

28 Then said Jesus unto them, When ye have lifted up the Son of man, then shall ye know that I am he, and that I do nothing of myself'; but as my Father hath taught me, I speak these things.

29 And he that sent me is with me: the Father hath not left me alone'; for I do always those things that please him.

30 As he spake these words, many believed on him.

31 Then said Jesus to those Jews which be-

lieved' on him, If ye contin'ue in my word, then are ye my disci'ples indeed';

32 And ye shall know the truth, and the . truth shall make you free.

33 ¶ They answered him, We be Abraham's seed, and were never in bondage to any man: how sayest thou, Ye shall be made free?

34 Jesus answered them, Verily, verily, I say unto you, Whosoev'er commit'teth sin is the servant of sin.

35 And the servant abid'eth not in the house for ever: but the Son abid'eth ever.

36 ·If the Son therefore shall make you free, ye shall be free indeed'.

37 I know that ye are Abraham's seed; but ye seek to kill me, because' my word hath no place in you.

38 I speak that which I have seen with my Father: and ye do that which ye have seen with your father.

39 They answered and said unto him, Abraham is ·our father. Jesus saith unto them, If ye were Abraham's children, ye would do the works of Abraham.

40 But now ye seek to kill me, a man that hath told you the truth, which I have heard of God: this did not Abraham.

41 Ye do the deeds of your father. Then said they to him, We be not born of fornica'- tion; we have one Father, even God.

42 Jesus said unto them, If God were your

Father, ye would love me: for I proceed'ed forth and came from God; neither came I of myself', but he sent me.

43 Why do ye not understand' my speech? even because' ye cannot hear my word.

44 Ye are of your father the devil, and the lusts of your father ye will do: he was a murderer from the begin'ning, and abode' not in the truth, because' there is no truth in him. When he speaketh a lie, he speaketh of his own: for he is a liar, and the father of it.

45 And because' I tell you the truth, ye be-lieve' me not.

46 Which of you convinc'eth me of sin? And if I say the truth, why do ye not believe' me?

47 He that is of God heareth God's words: ye therefore hear them not, because' ye are not of God.

48 Then answered the Jews, and said unto him, Say we not well that thou art a Samar'i-tan, and hast a devil?

49 Jesus answered, I have not a devil; but I honor my Father, and ye do dishon'or me.

50 And I seek not mine own glory: there is one that seeketh and judgeth.

51 Verily, verily, I say unto you, If a man keep my saying, he shall never see death.

52 Then said the Jews unto him, Now we know that thou hast a devil. Abraham is dead, and the prophets; and thou sayest, If a

man keep my saying, he shall never taste of death.

53 Art thou greater than our father Abraham, which is dead? and the prophets are dead: whom makest thou thyself?

54 Jesus answered, If I honor myself, my honor is nothing: it is my Father that honoreth me; of whom ye say, that he is your God:

55 Yet ye have not known him; but I know him: and if I should say, I know him not, I shall be a liar like unto you: but I know him, and keep his saying.

56 Your father Abraham rejoiced to see my day: and he saw it, and was glad.

57 Then said the Jews unto him, Thou art not yet fifty years old, and hast thou seen Abraham?

58 Jesus said unto them, Verily, verily, I say unto you, Before Abraham was, I am.

59 Then took they up stones to cast at him: but Jesus hid himself, and went out of the temple, going through the midst of them, and so passed by.

CHAPTER IX.

1 And as Jesus passed by, he saw a man which was blind from his birth.

2 And his disci'ples asked him, saying, Master, who did sin, this man, or his parents, that he was born blind?

3 Jesus answered, Neither hath this man

sinned, nor his parents: but that the works of God should be made manifest in him.

4 I must work the works of him that sent me, while it is day: the night cometh, when no man can work.

5 As long as I am in the world, I am the light of the world.

6 When he had thus spoken, he spat on the ground, and made clay of the spittle, and he anoint'ed the eyes of the blind man with the clay,

7 And said unto him, Go, wash in the pool of Silo'am, (which is by inter'preta'tion, Sent.) He went his way therefore, and washed, and came seeing.

8 ¶ The neighbors therefore, and they which before' had seen him that he was blind, said, Is not this he that sat and begged?

9 Some said, This is he: others said, He is like him: but he said, I am he.

10 Therefore said they unto him, How were thine eyes opened?

11 He answered and said, A man that is called Jesus made clay, and anoint'ed mine eyes, and said unto me, Go to the pool of Silo'am, and wash: and I went and washed, and I received' sight.

12 Then said they unto him, Where is he? He said, I know not.

13 ¶ They brought to the Pharisees him that afore'time was blind.

14 And it was the sabbath day when Jesus made the clay, and opened his eyes.

15 Then again' the Pharisees also asked him how he had received' his sight. He said unto them, He put clay upon' mine eyes, and I washed, and do see.

· 16 Therefore said some of the Pharisees, This man is not of God, because' he keepeth not the sabbath day. Others said, How can a man that is a sinner do such miracles? And there was a divis'ion among' them.

17 They say unto the blind man again', What sayest thou of him, that he hath opened thine eyes? He said, He is a prophet.

18 But the Jews did not believe' concern'ing him, that he had been blind, and received' his sight, until' they called the parents of him that had received' his sight.

19 And they asked them, saying, Is this your son, who ye say was born blind? how then doth he now see?

20 His parents answered them and said, We know that this is our son, and that he was born blind:

21 But by what means he now seeth, we know not; or who hath opened his eyes, we know not: he is of age; ask him: he shall speak for himself'.

22 These words spake his parents, because' they feared the Jews: for the Jews had agreed' alread'y, that if any man did confess' that he was

Christ, he should be put out of the synagogue.

23 Therefore said his parents, He is of age;
ask him.

24 Then again' called they the man that was
blind, and said unto him, Give God the praise:
we know that this man is a sinner.

25 He answered and said, Whether he be a
sinner or no, I know not: one thing I know,
that, whereas I was blind, now I see.

26 Then said they to him again', What did
he to thee? how opened he thine eyes?

27 He answered them, I have told you alread'y, and ye did not hear: wharefore would
ye hear it again'? will ye also be his disci'ples?

28 Then they reviled' him, and said, Thou
art his disci'ple; but we are Moses' disci'ples.

29 We know that God spake unto Moses: as
for this fellow, we know not from whence he is.

30 The man answered and said unto them,
Why herein' is a marvelous thing, that ye know
not from whence he is, and yet he hath opened
mine eyes.

31 Now we know that God heareth not sin-
ners: but if any man be a worshiper of God,
and doeth his will, him he heareth.

32 Since the world began' was it not heard
that any man opened the eyes of one that was
born blind.

33 If this man were not of God, he could do
nothing.

34 They answered and said unto him, Thou wast altogeth'er born in sins, and dost thou teach us? And they cast him out.

35 Jesus heard that they had cast him out; and when he had found him, he said unto him, Dost thou believe' on the Son of God?

36 He answered and said, Who is he, Lord, that I might believe' on him?

37 And Jesus said unto him, Thou hast both seen him, and it is he that talketh with thee.

38 And he said, Lord, I believe'. And he worshiped him.

39 ¶ And Jesus said, For judgment I am come into this world, that they which see not might see; and that they which see might be made blind.

40 And some of the Pharisees which were with him heard these words, and said unto him, Are we blind also?

41 Jesus said unto them, If ye were blind, ye should have no sin: but now ye say, We see; therefore your sin remain'eth.

CHAPTER X.

1 Verily, verily, I say unto you, He that en-tereth not by the door into the sheepfold, but climbeth up some other way, the same is a thief and a robber.

2 But he that entereth in by the door is the shepherd of the sheep.

3 To him the porter openeth; and the sheep hear his voice: and he calleth his own sheep by name, and leadeth them out.

4 And when he putteth forth his own sheep, he goeth before' them, and the sheep follow him: for they know his voice.

5 And a stranger will they not follow, but will flee from him; for they know not the voice of strangers.

6 This parable spake Jesus unto them; but they understood' not what things they were which he spake unto them.

7 Then said Jesus unto them again', Verily, verily, I say unto you, I am the door of the sheep.

8 All that ever came before' me are thieves and robbers: but the sheep did not hear them.

9 I am the door: by me if any man enter in, he shall be saved, and shall go in and out, and find pasture.

10 The thief cometh not, but for to steal, and to kill, and to destroy': I am come that they might have life, and that they might have it more abun'dantly.

11 I am the good shepherd: the good shepherd giveth his life for the sheep.

12 But he that is a hireling, and not the shepherd, whose own the sheep are not, seeth the wolf coming, and leaveth the sheep, and fleeth; and the wolf catcheth them, and scattereth the sheep.

13 The hireling fleeth, because' he is a hireling, and careth not for the sheep.

14 I am the good shepherd, and know my sheep, and am known of mine.

15 As the Father knoweth me, even so know I the Father: and I lay down my life for the sheep.

16 And other sheep I have, which are not of this fold: them also I must bring, and they shall hear my voice; and there shall be one fold, and one shepherd.

17 Therefore doth my Father love me, because' I lay down my life, that I might take it again'.

18 No man taketh it from me, but I lay it down of myself'. I have power to lay it down, and I have power to take it again'. This command'ment have I received' of my Father.

19 ¶ There was a divis'ion therefore again' among' the Jews for these sayings.

20 And many of them said, He hath a devil, and is mad; why hear ye him?

21 Others said, These are not the words of him that hath a devil. Can a devil open the eyes of the blind?

22 ¶ And it was at Jeru'salem the feast of the dedica'tion, and it was winter.

23 And Jesus walked in the temple in Solomon's porch.

24 Then came the Jews round about' him, and said unto him, How long dost thou make us

to doubt? If thou be the Christ, tell us plainly.

25 Jesus answered them, I told you, and ye believed' not: the works that I do in my Father's name, they bear witness of me.

26 But ye believe' not, because' ye are not of my sheep, as I said unto you.

27 My sheep hear my voice, and I know them, and they follow me:

28 And I give unto them eter'nal life; and they shall never perish, neither shall any man pluck them out of my hand.

29 My Father, which gave them me, is greater than all; and no man is able to pluck them out of my Father's hand.

30 I and my Father are one.

31 Then the Jews took up stones again' to stone him.

32 Jesus answered them, Many good works have I shewed you from my Father; for which of those works do ye stone me?

33 The Jews answered him, saying, For a good work we stone thee not; but for blasphemy; and because' that thou, being a man, makest thyself' God.

34 Jesus answered them, Is it not written in your law, I said, Ye are gods?

35 If he called them gods, unto whom the word of God came, and the Scripture cannot be broken;

36 Say ye of him, whom the Father hath

sanctified, and sent into the world, Thou blas-
phem'est; because' I·said, I am the Son of
God?

37 If I do not the works of my Father, believe' me not.

38 But if I do, though ye believe' not me,
believe' the works; that ye ·may know, and
believe', that the Father is in me, and I in him.

39 Therefore they sought again' to take him;
but he escaped' out of their hand,

40 And went away' again' beyond' Jordan
into the place where John at first baptized';
and there he abode'.

41 And many resort'ed unto him, and said,
John did no miracle: but all things that John
spake of this man were true.

42 And many believed' on him there.

CHAPTER XI.

1 Now a certain man was sick, named Lazarus, of Bethany, the town of Mary and her
sister Martha.

2 (It was that Mary which anoint'ed the Lord
with ointment, and wiped his feet with her
hair, whose brother Lazarus was sick.)

3 Therefore his sisters sent unto him, saying,
Lord, behold', he whom thou lovest is sick.

4 When Jesus heard that, he said, This sick-
ness is not unto death, but for the glory of
God, that the Son of God might be glorified
thereby'.

5 Now Jesus loved Martha, and her sister, and Lazarus.

6 When he had heard therefore that he was sick, he abode' two days still in the same place where he was.

7 Then after that saith he to his disci'ples, Let us go into Jude'a again'.

8 His disci'ples say unto him, Master, the Jews of late sought to stone thee; and goest thou thither again'?

9 Jesus answered, Are there not twelve hours in the day? If any man walk in the day, he stumbleth not, because' he seeth the light of this world.

10 But if a man walk in the night, he stumbleth, because' there is no light in him.

11 These things said he: and after that he saith unto them, Our friend Lazarus sleepeth; but I go, that I may awake' him out of sleep.

12 Then said his disci'ples, Lord, if he sleep, he shall do well.

13 Howbe'it Jesus spake of his death: but they thought that he had spoken of taking of rest in sleep.

14 Then said Jesus unto them plainly, Lazarus is dead.

15 And I am glad for your sakes that I was not there, to the intent' ye may believe'; nevertheless' let us go unto him.

16 Then said Thomas, which is called Didy-

mus, unto his fellow disci'ples, Let us also go, that we may die with him.

17 Then when Jesus came, he found that he had lain in the grave four days alread'y.

18 Now Bethany was nigh unto Jeru'salem, about' fifteen furlongs off:

19 And many of the Jews came to Martha and Mary, to comfort them concern'ing their brother.

20 Then Martha, as soon as she heard that Jesus was coming, went and met him: but Mary sat still in the house.

21 Then said Martha unto Jesus, Lord, if thou hadst been here, my brother had not died.

22 But I know, that even now, whatsoev'er thou wilt ask of God, God will give it thee.

23 Jesus saith unto her, Thy brother shall rise again'.

24 Martha saith unto him, I know that he shall rise again' in the resurrec'tion at the last day.

25 Jesus said unto her, I am the resurrec'tion, and the life: he that believ'eth in me, though he were dead, yet shall he live:

26 And whosoev'er liveth and believ'eth in me shall never die. Believ'est thou this?

27 She saith unto him, Yea, Lord: I believe' that thou art the Christ, the Son of God, which should come into the world.

28 And when she had so said, she went her way, and called Mary her sister secretly,

saying, The Master is come, and calleth for thee.

29 As soon as she heard that, she arose' quickly, and came unto him.

30 Now Jesus was not yet come into the town, but was in that place where Martha met him.

31 The Jews then which were with her in the house, and comforted her, when they saw Mary, that she rose up hastily and went out, followed her, saying, She goeth unto the grave to weep there.

32 Then when Mary was come where Jesus was, and saw him, she fell down at his feet, saying unto him, Lord, if thou hadst been here, my brother had not died.

33 When Jesus therefore saw her weeping, and the Jews also weeping which came with her, he groaned in the spirit, and was troubled,

34 And said, Where have ye laid him? They say unto him, Lord, come and see.

35 Jesus wept.

36 Then said the Jews, Behold' how he loved him!

37 And some of them said, Could not this man, which opened the eyes of the blind, have caused that even this man should not have died?

38 Jesus therefore again' groaning in himself' cometh to the grave. It was a cave, and a stone lay upon' it.

39 Jesus said, Take ye away' the stone. Martha, the sister of him that was dead, saith unto him, Lord, by this time he stinketh: for he hath been dead four days.

40 Jesus saith unto her, Said I not unto thee, that, if thou wouldest believe', thou shouldest see the glory of God?

41 Then they took away' the stone from the place where the dead was laid. And Jesus lifted up his eyes, and said, Father, I thank thee that thou hast heard me.

42 And I knew that thou hearest me always: but because' of the people which stand by I said it, that they may believe' that thou hast sent me.

43 And when he thus had spoken, he cried with a loud voice, Lazarus, come forth.

44 And he that was dead came forth, bound hand and foot with grave-clothes; and his face was bound about' with a napkin. Jesus saith unto them, Loose him, and let him go.

45 Then many of the Jews which came to Mary, and had seen the things which Jesus did, believed' on him.

46 But some of them went their ways to the Pharisees, and told them what things Jesus had done.

47 ¶ Then gathered the chief priests and the Pharisees a council, and said, What do we? for this man doeth many miracles.

48 If we let him thus alone', all men will be-

lieve' on him; and the Romans shall come and take away' both our place and nation.

49 And one of them, named Caiapfias, being the high priest that same year, said unto them, Ye know nothing at all,

50 Nor consid'er that it is expe'dient for us, that one man should die for the people, and that the whole nation perish not.

51 And this spake he not of himself': but being high priest that year, he propfiesied that Jesus should die for that nation;

52 And not for that nation only, but that also he should gather togeth'er in one the children of God that were scattered abroad'.

53 Then from that day forth they took coun-sel togeth'er for to put him to death.

54 Jesus therefore walked no more openly among' the Jews; but went thence unto a country near to the wilderness, into a city called Epfiraim, and there contin'ued with his disci'ples.

55 ¶ And the Jews' passover was nigh at hand: and many went out of the country up to Jeru'salem before' the passover, to purify themselves'.

56 Then sought they for Jesus, and spake among' themselves', as they stood in the tem-ple, What think ye, that he will not come to the feast?

57 Now both the chief priests and the Pfari-sees had given a command'ment, that, if any

man knew whare he were, he should shew it, that they might take him.

CHAPTER XII.

1 Then Jesus six days before' the passover came to Bethany, whare Lazarus was which had been dead, whom he raised from the dead.

2 Thare they made him a supper; and Martha served: but Lazarus was one of them that sat at the table with him.

3 Then took Mary a pound of ointment of spikenard, very costly, and anoint'ed the feet of Jesus, and wiped his feet with her hair: and the house was filled with the odor of the ointment.

4 Then saith one of his disci'ples, Judas Iscar'iot, Simon's son, which should betray' him,

5 Why was not this ointment sold for three hundred pence, and given to the poor?

6 This he said, not that he cared for the poor; but because' he was a thief, and had the bag, and bare what was put therein'.

7 Then said Jesus, Let her alone': against' the day of my burying hath she kept this.

8 For the poor always ye have with you; but me ye have not always.

9 Much people of the Jews therefore knew that he was thare: and they came not for Jesus' sake only, but that they might see Lazarus also, whom he had raised from the dead.

10 ¶ But the chief priests consult'ed that they might put Lazarus also to death;

11 Because' that by reason of him many of the Jews went away', and believed' on Jesus.

12 ¶ On the next day much people that were come to the feast, when they heard that Jesus was coming to Jeru'salem,

13 Took branches of palm trees, and went forth to meet him, and cried, Hosan'na: Blessed is the King of Israel that cometh in the name of the Lord.

14 And Jesus, when he had found a young ass, sat thereon'; as it is written,

15 Fear not, daughter of Sion: behold', thy King cometh, sitting on an ass's colt.

16 These things understood' not his disci'ples at the first: but when Jesus was glorified, then remembered they that these things were written of him, and that they had done these things unto him.

17 The people therefore that was with him when he called Lazarus out of his grave, and raised him from the dead, bare record.

18 For this cause the people also met him, for that they heard that he had done this miracle.

19 The Pharisees therefore said among' themselves', Perceive' ye how ye prevail' nothing? behold', the world is gone after him.

20 ¶ And there were certain Greeks among' them that came up to worship at the feast:

21 The same came therefore to Phlip, which was of Bethsa'ida of Galilee, and desired' him, saying, Sir, we would see Jesus.

22 Philip cometh and telleth Andrew: and again' Andrew and Philip tell Jesus.

23 ¶ And Jesus answered them, saying, The hour is come, that the Son of man should be glorified.

24 Verily, verily, I say unto you, Except' a corn of wheat fall into the ground and die, it abid'eth alone': but if it die, it bringeth forth much fruit.

25 He that loveth his life shall lose it; and he that hateth his life in this world shall keep it unto life eter'nal.

26 If any man serve me, let him follow me; and where I am, there shall also my servant be: if any man serve me, him will my Father honor.

27 Now is my soul troubled; and what shall I say? Father, save me from this hour: but for this cause came I unto this hour.

28 Father, glorify thy name. Then came there a voice from heaven, saying, I have both glorified it, and will glorify it again'.

29 The people therefore that stood by, and heard it, said that it thundered: others said, An angel spake to him.

30 Jesus answered and said, This voice came not because' of me, but for your sakes.

31 Now is the judgment of this world:

now shall the prince of this world be cast out.

32 And I, if I be lifted up from the earth. will draw all men unto me.

33 This he said, signifying what death he should die.

34 The people answered him, We have heard out of the law that Christ abid'eth for ever: and how sayest thou, The Son of man must be lifted up? who is this Son of man?

35 Then Jesus said unto them, Yet a little while is the light with you. Walk while ye have the light, lest darkness come upon' you: for he that walketh in darkness knoweth not whither he goeth.

36 While ye have light, believe' in the light, that ye may be the children of light. These things spake Jesus, and depart'ed, and did hide himself' from them.

37 ¶ But though he had done so many miracles before' them, yet they believed' not on him:

38 That the saying of Esai'as the prophet might be fulfilled', which he spake, Lord, who hath believed' our report? and to whom hath the arm of the Lord been revealed'?

39 Therefore they could not believe', because' that Esai'as said again',

40 He hath blinded their eyes, and hardened their heart; that they should not see with their eyes, nor understand' with their heart, and be convert'ed, and I should heal them.

41 These things said Esai'as, when he saw his glory, and spake of him.

42 ¶ Nevertheless' among' the chief rulers also many believed' on him; but because' of the Pharisees they did not confess' him, lest they should be put out of the synagogue:

43 For they loved the praise of men more than the praise of God.

44 ¶ Jesus cried and said, He that believ'eth on me, believ'eth not on me, but on him that sent me.

45 And he that seeth me seeth him that sent me.

46 I am come a light into the world, that whosoev'er believ'eth on me should not abide' in darkness.

47 And if any man hear my words, and believe' not, I judge him not: for I came not to judge the world, but to save the world.

48 He that reject'eth me, and receiv'eth not my words, hath one that judgeth him: the word that I have spoken, the same shall judge him in the last day.

49 For I have not spoken of myself'; but the Father which sent me, he gave me a command'ment, what I should say, and what I should speak.

50 And I know that his command'ment is life everlast'ing: whatsoev'er I speak therefore, even as the Father said unto me, so I speak.

CHAPTER XIII.

1 Now before' the feast of the passover, when Jesus knew that his hour was come that he should depart' out of this world unto the Father, having loved his own which were in the world, he loved them unto the end.

2 And supper being ended, the devil having now put into the heart of Judas Iscar'iot, Simon's son, to betray' him;

3 Jesus knowing that the Father had given all things into his hands, and that he was come from God, and went to God;

4 He riseth from supper, and laid aside' his garments; and took a towel, and girded himself'.

5 After that he poureth water into a basin, and began' to wash the disci'ples' feet, and to wipe them with the towel wharewith' he was girded.

6 Then cometh he to Simon Peter: and Peter saith unto him, Lord, dost thou wash my feet?

7 Jesus answered and said unto him, What I do thou knowest not now; but thou shalt know hereaft'er.

8 Peter saith unto him, Thou shalt never wash my feet. Jesus answered him, If I wash thee not, thou hast no part with me.

9 Simon Peter saith unto him, Lord, not my feet only, but also my hands and my head.

10 Jesus saith to him, He that is washed

needeth not save to wash his feet, but is clean every whit: and ye are clean, but not all.

11 For he knew who should betray' him; therefore said he, Ye are not all clean.

12 So after he had washed their feet, and had taken his garments, and was set down again', he said unto them, Know ye what I have done to you?

13 Ye call me Master and Lord: and ye say well; for so I am.

14 If I then, your Lord and Master, have washed your feet; ye also ought to wash one anoth'er's feet.

15 For I have given you an exam'ple, that ye should do as I have done to you.

16 Verily, verily, I say unto you, The servant is not greater than his lord; neither he that is sent greater than he that sent him.

17 If ye know these things, happy are ye if ye do them.

18 ¶ I speak not of you all: I know whom I have chosen: but that the Scripture may be fulfilled', He that eateth bread with me hath lifted up his heel against' me.

19 Now I tell you before' it come, that, when it is come to pass, ye may believe' that I am he.

20 Verily, verily, I say unto you, He that re-ceiv'eth whomsoev'er I send receiv'eth me; and he that receiveth me receiv'eth him that sent me.

21 When Jesus had thus said, he was

troubled in spirit, andtestified, and said, Verily, verily, I say unto you, that one of you shall
betray' me.

22 Then the disci'ples looked one on anoth'-
er, doubting of whom he spake.

23 Now there was leaning on Jesus' bosom
one of his disci'ples, whom Jesus loved.

24 Simon Peter therefore beckoned to him,
that he should ask who it should be of whom
he spake.

25 He then lying on Jesus' breast saith unto him, Lord, who is it?

26 Jesus answered, He it is, to whom I shall
give a sop, when I have dipped it.   And when
he had dipped the sop, he gave it to Judas
Iscar'iot, the son of Simon.

27 And after the sop Satan entered into
him.   Then said Jesus unto him, That thou
doest, do quickly.

28 Now no man at the table knew for what
intent' he spake this unto him.

29 For some of them thought, because' Judas had the bag, that Jesus had said unto him,
Buy those things that we have need of against'
the feast; or, that he should give something to
the poor.

30 He then, having received' the sop, went
imme'diately out; and it was night.

31 ¶ Therefore, when he was gone out, Jesus said, Now is the Son of man glorified, and
God is glorified in him.

·32 If God be glorified in him, God shall also glorify him in himself', and shall straightway glorify him.

33 Little children, yet a little while I am with you. Ye shall seek me; and as I said unto the Jews, Whither I go, ye cannot come; so now I say to you.

34 A new command'ment I give unto you, That ye love one anoth'er; as I have loved you, that ye also love one anoth'er.

35 By this shall all men know that ye are my disci'ples, if ye have love one to anoth'er.

36 ¶ Simon Peter said unto him, Lord, whither goest thou? Jesus answered him, Whither I go, thou canst not follow me now; but thou shalt follow me afterwards.

37 Peter said unto him, Lord, why cannot I follow thee now? I will lay down my life for thy sake.

38 Jesus answered him, Wilt thou lay down thy life for my sake? Verily, verily, I say unto thee, The cock shall not crow, till thou hast denied' me thrice.

CHAPTER XIV.

1 Let not your heart be troubled: ye believe' in God, believe' also in me.

2 In my Father's house are many mansions: if it were not so, I would have told you. I go to prepare' a place for you.

3 And if I go and prepare' a place for you,

I will come again', and receive' you unto myself'; that where I am, there ye may be also.

4 And whither I go ye know, and the way ye know.

5 Thomas saith unto him, Lord, we know not whither thou goest; and how can we know the way?

6 Jesus saith unto him, I am the way, the truth, and the life: no man cometh unto the Father, but by me.

7 If ye had known me, ye should have known my Father also: and from henceforth' ye know him, and have seen him.

8 Pfiilip saith unto him, Lord, shew us the Father, and it suffic'eth us.

9 Jesus saith unto him, Have I been so long time with you, and yet hast thou nòt known me, Pfiilip? he that hath seen me hath seen the Father; and how sayest thou then, Shew us the Father?

10 Believ'est thou not that I am in the Father, and the Father in me? the words that I speak unto you I speak not of myself': but the Father that dwelleth in me, he doeth the works.

11 Believe' me that I am in the Father, and the Father in me: or else believe' me for the very works' sake.

12 Verily, verily, I say unto you, He that believ'eth on me, the works that I do shall he

do also; and greater works than these shall he do; because' I go unto my Father.

13 And whatsoev'er ye shall ask in my name, that will I do, that the Father may be glorified in the Son.

14 If ye shall ask anything in my name, I will do it.

15 ¶ If ye love me, keep my command'ments.

16 And I will pray the Father, and he shall give you anoth'er Comforter, that he may abide' with you for ever;

17 Even the Spirit of truth; whom the world cannot receive', because' it seeth him not, neither knoweth him: but ye know him; for he dwelleth with you, and shall be in you.

18 I will not leave you comfortless: I will come to you.

19 Yet a little while, and the world seeth me no more; but ye see me: because' I live, ye shall live also.

20 At that day ye shall know that I am in my Father, and ye in me, and I in you.

21 He that hath my command'ments, and keepeth them, he it is that loveth me: and he that loveth me shall be loved of my Father, and I will love him, and will manifest myself' to him.

22 Judas saith unto him, not Iscar'iot, Lord, how is it that thou wilt manifest thyself' unto us, and not unto the world?

23 Jesus answered and said unto him, If a

man love me, he will keep my words: and my Father will love him, and we will come unto him, and make our abode' with him.

24 He that loveth me not keepeth not my sayings: and the word which ye hear is not mine, but the Father's which sent me.

25 These things have I spoken unto you, being yet present-with you.

26 But the Comforter, which is the Holy Ghost, whom the Father will send in my name, he shall teach you all things, and bring all things to your remem'brance, whatsoev'er I have said unto you.

27 Peace I leave with you, my peace I give unto you: not as the world giveth, give I unto you. Let not your heart be troubled, neither let it be afraid'.

28 Ye have heard how I said unto you, I go away', and come again' unto you. If ye loved me, ye would rejoice, because' I said, I go unto the Father: for my Father is greater than I.

29 And now I have told you before' it come to pass, that, when it is come to pass, ye might 'believe'.

30 Hereaft'er I will not talk much with you: for the prince of this world cometh, and hath nothing in me.

31 But that the world may know that I love the Father; and as the Father gave me command'ment, even so I do. Arise', let us go hence.

CHAPTER XV.

1 I am the true vine, and my Father is the husbandman.

2 Every branch in me that beareth not fruit he taketh away': and every branch that beareth fruit, he purgeth it, that it may bring forth more fruit.

3 Now ye are clean through the word which I have spoken unto you.

4 Abide' in me, and I in you. As the branch cannot bear fruit of itself', except' it abide' in the vine; no more can ye, except' ye abide' in me.

5 I am the vine, ye are the branches. He that abid'eth in me, and I in him, the same bringeth forth much fruit; for without' me ye can do nothing.

6 If a man abide' not in me, he is cast forth as a branch, and is withered; and men gather them, and cast them into the fire, and they are burned.

7 If ye abide' in me, and my words abide' in you, ye shall ask what ye will, and it shall be done unto you.

8 Herein' is my Father glorified, that ye bear much fruit; so shall ye be my disci'ples.

9 As the Father hath loved me, so have I loved you: contin'ue ye in my love.

10 If ye keep my command'ments, ye shall abide' in my love; even as I have kept

my Father's command'ments, and abide' in his love.

11 These things have I spoken unto you, that my joy might remain' in you, and that your joy might be full.

12 This is my command'ment, That ye love one anoth'er, as I have loved you.

13 Greater love hath no man than this, that a man lay down his life for his friends.

14 Ye are my friends, if ye do whatsoev'er I command' you.

15 Henceforth' I call you not servants; for the servant knoweth not what his lord doeth: but I have called you friends; for all things that I have heard of my Father I have made known unto you.

16 Ye have not chosen me, but I have chosen you, and ordained' you, that ye should go and bring forth fruit, and that your fruit should remain'; that whatsoev'er ye shall ask of the Father in my name, he may give it you.

17 These things I command' you, that ye love one anoth'er.

18 If the world hate you, ye know that it hated me before' it hated you.

19 If ye were of the world, the world would love his own; but because' ye are not of the world, but I have chosen you out of the world, therefore the world hateth you.

20 Remem'ber the word that I said unto you, The servant is not greater than his lord. If

thay have persecuted me, thay will also persecute you; if thay have kept my saying, thay
will keep yours also.

21 But all these things will thay do unto
you for my name's sake, because' thay know
not him that sent me.

22 If I had not come and spoken unto them,
thay had not had sin; but now thay have no
cloak for their sin.

23 He that hateth me hateth my Father also.

24 If I had not done among' them the works
which none other man did, thay had not had
sin: but now have thay both seen and hated
both me and my Father.

25 But this cometh to pass, that the word
might be fulfilled' that is written in their law,
Thay hated me without' a cause.   .

26 But when the Comforter is come, whom
I will send unto you from the Father, even
the Spirit of truth, which proceed'eth from the
Father, he shall testify of me:

27 And ye also shall bear witness, because'
ye have been with me from the begin'ning.

CHAPTER XVI.

1 These things have I spoken unto you, that
ye should not be offend'ed.

2 Thay shall put you out of the synagogues:
yea, the time cometh, that whosoev'er killeth
you will think that he doeth God service.

3 And these things will thay do unto you,

because' they have not known the Father, nor me.

4 But these things have I told you, that when the time shall come, ye may remem'ber that I told you of them. And these things I said not unto you at the begin'ning, because' I was with you.

5 But now I go my way to him that sent me; and none of you asketh me, Whither goest thou?

6 But because' I have said these things unto you, sorrow hath filled your heart.

7 Nevertheless' I tell you the truth; It is expe'dient for you that I go away': for if I go not away', the Comforter will not come unto you; but if I depart', I will send him unto you.

8 And when he is come, he will reprove' the world of sin, and of righteousness, and of judgment:

9 Of sin, because' they believe' not on me;

10 Of righteousness, because' I go to my Father, and ye see me no more;

11 Of judgment, because' the prince of this world is judged.

12 I have yet many things to say unto you, but ye cannot bear them now.

13 Howbe'it when he, the Spirit of truth, is' come, he will guide you into all truth: for he shall not speak of himself'; but whatsoev'er he shall hear, that shall he speak: and he will shew you things to come.

14 He shall glorify me: for he shall receive' of mine, and shall shew it unto you.

15 All things that the Father hath are mine: therefore said I, that he shall take of mine, and shall shew it unto you.

16 A little while, and ye shall not see me: and again', a little while, and ye shall see me, because' I go to the Father.

17 Then said some of his disci'ples among' themselves', What is this that he saith unto us, A little while, and ye shall not see me: and again', a little while, and ye shall see me: and, Because' I go to the Father?

18 They said therefore, What is this that he saith, A little while? we cannot tell what he saith.

19 Now Jesus knew that they were desir'ous to ask him, and said unto them, Do ye inquire' among' yourselves' of that I said, A little while, and ye shall not see me: and again', a little while, and ye shall see me?

20 Verily, verily, I say unto you, That ye shall weep and lament', but the world shall rejoice'; and ye shall be sorrowful, but your sorrow shall be turned into joy.

21 A woman when she is in travail hath sorrow, because' her hour is come: but as soon as she is deliv'ered of the child, she remem'- bereth no more the anguish, for joy that a man is born into the world.

22 And ye now therefore have sorrow; but I

will see you again', and your heart shall rejoice', and your joy no man taketh from you.

23 And in that day ye shall ask me nothing. Verily, verily, I say unto you, Whatsoev'er ye shall ask the Father in my name, he will give it you.

24 Hitherto' have ye asked nothing in my name: ask, and ye shall receive', that your joy may be full.

25 These things have I spoken unto you in proverbs: but the time cometh, when I shall no more speak unto you in proverbs, but I shall shew you plainly of the Father.

26 At that day ye shall ask in my name: and I say not unto you, that I will pray the Father for you:

27 For the Father himself' loveth you, because' ye have loved me, and have believed' that I came out from God.

28 I came forth from the Father, and am come into the world: again', I leave the world, and go to the Father.

29 His disci'ples said unto him, Lo, now speakest thou plainly, and speakest no proverb.

30 Now are we sure that thou knowest all things, and needest not that any man should ask thee: by this we believe' that thou camest forth from God.

31 Jesus answered them, Do ye now believe'?

32 Behold', the hour cometh, yea, is now come, that ye shall be scattered, every man to

his own, and shall leave me alone': and yet I am not alone', because' the Father is with me.

33 These things I have spoken unto you, that in me ye might have peace. In the world ye shall have tribula'tion: but be of good cheer; I have overcome' the world.

CHAPTER XVII.

1 These words spake Jesus, and lifted up his eyes to heaven, and said, Father, the hour is come; glorify thy Son, that thy Son also may glorify thee:

2 As thou hast given him power over all flesh, that he should give eter'nal life to as many as thou hast given him.

3 And this is life eter'nal, that they might know thee the only true God, and Jesus Christ, whom thou hast sent.

4 I have glorified thee on the earth: I have finished the work which thou gavest me to do.

5 And now, O Father, glorify thou me with thine own self with the glory which I had with thee before' the world was.

6 I have manifested thy name unto the men which thou gavest me out of the world: thine they were, and thou gavest them me; and they have kept thy word.

7 Now they have known that all things whatsoev'er thou hast given me are of thee.

8 For I have given unto them the words which thou gavest me; and they have re-

ceived' them, and have known surely that I came out from thee, and they have believed' that thou didst send me.

9 I pray for them: I pray not for the world, but for them which thou hast given me; for they are thine.

10 And all mine are thine, and thine are mine; and I am glorified in them.

11 And now I am no more in the world, but these are in the world, and I come to thee. Holy Father, keep through thine own name those whom thou hast given me, that they may be one, as we are.

12 While I was with them in the world, I kept them in thy name: those that thou gav-est me I have kept, and none of them is lost, but the son of perdi'tion; that the Scripture might be fulfilled'.

13 And now come I to thee; and these things I speak in the world, that they might have my joy fulfilled' in themselves'.

14 I have given them thy word; and the world hath hated them, because' they are not of the world, even as I am not of the world.

15 I pray not that thou shouldest take them out of the world, but that thou shouldest keep them from the evil.

16 They are not of the world, even as I am not of the world.

17 Sanctify them through thy truth: thy word is truth.

18 As thou hast sent me into the world, even so have I also sent them into the world.

19 And for their sakes I sanctify myself', that they also might be sanctified through the truth.

20 Neither pray I for these alone', but for them also which shall believe' on me through their word;

21 That they all may be one; as thou, Father, art in me, and I in thee, that they also may be one in us: that the world may believe' that thou hast sent me.

22 And the glory which thou gavest me I have given them; that they may be one, even as we are one:

23 I in them, and thou in me, that they may be made perfect in one; and that the world may know that thou hast sent me, and hast loved them, as thou hast loved me.

24 Father, I will that they also, whom thou hast given me, be with me where I am; that they may behold' my glory, which thou hast given me: for thou lovedst me before' the founda'tion of the world.

25 O righteous Father, the world hath not known thee: but I have known thee, and these have known that thou hast sent me.

26 And I have declared' unto them thy name, and will declare' it; that the love wherewith' thou hast loved me may be in them, and I in them.

CHAPTER XVIII.

1 When Jesus had spoken these words, he went forth with his disci'ples over the brook Cedron, where was a garden, into the which he entered, and his disci'ples.

2 And Judas also, which betrayed' him, knew the place: for Jesus ofttimes resort'ed thither with his disci'ples.

3 Judas then, having received' a band of men and officers from the chief priests and Pharisees, cometh thither with lanterns and torches and weapons.

4 Jesus therefore, knowing all things that should come upon' him, went forth, and said unto them, Whom seek ye?

5 They answered him, Jesus of Nazareth. Jesus saith unto them, I am he. And Judas also, which betrayed' him, stood with them.

6 As soon then as he had said unto them, I am he, they went backward, and fell to the ground.

7 Then asked he them again', Whom seek ye? And they said, Jesus of Nazareth.

8 Jesus answered, I have told you that I am he: if therefore ye seek me, let these go their way:

9 That the saying might be fulfilled', which he spake, Of them which thou gavest me have I lost none.

10 Then Simon Peter having a sword drew

it, and smote the high priest's servant, and cut off his right ear. The servant's name was Malchus.

11 Then said Jesus unto Peter, Put up thy sword into the sheath: the cup which my Father hath given me, shall I not drink it?

12 Then, the band and the captain and officers of the Jews took Jesus, and bound him,

13 And led him away' to Annas first; for he was father in law to Caiaphas, which was the high priest that same year.

14 Now Caiaphas was he, which gave counsel to the Jews, that it was expe'dient that one man should die for the people.

15 ¶ And Simon Peter followed Jesus, and so did anoth'er disci'ple: that disci'ple was known unto the high priest, and went in with Jesus into the palace of the high priest.

16 But Peter stood at the door without'. Then went out that other disci'ple, which was known unto the high priest, and spake unto her that kept the door, and brought in Peter.

17 Then saith the damsel that kept the door unto Peter, Art not thou also one of this man's disci'ples? He saith, I am not.

18 And the servants and officers stood there, who had made a fire of coals, for it was cold; and they warmed themselves': and Peter stood with them, and warmed himself'.

19 ¶ The high priest then asked Jesus of his disci'ples, and of his doctrine.

20 Jesus answered him, I spake openly to the world; I ever taught in the synagogue, and in the temple, whither the Jews always resort'; and in secret have I said nothing.

21 Why askest thou me? ask them which heard me, what I have said unto them: behold', they know what I said.

22 And when he had thus spoken, one of the officers which stood by struck Jesus with the palm of his hand, saying, Answerest thou the high priest so?

23 Jesus answered him, If I have spoken evil, bear witness of the evil: but if well, why smitest thou me? -

24 Now Annas had sent him bound unto Caiapfias the high priest.

25 And Simon Peter stood and warmed himself'. They said therefore unto him, Art not thou also one of his disci'ples? He denied' it, and said, I am not.

26 One of the servants of the high priest, being his kinsman whose ear Peter cut off, saith, Did not I see thee in the garden with him?

27 Peter then denied again'; and imme'diately the cock crew.

28 ¶ Then led they Jesus from Caiapfias unto the hall of judgment: and it was early; and they themselves' went not into the judg-. ment hall, lest they should be defiled'; but that they might eat the passover.

29 Pilate then went out unto them, and said, What accusa'tion bring ye against' this man?

30 They answered and said unto him, If he were not a malefac'tor, we would not have deliv'ered him up unto thee.

31 Then said Pilate unto them, Take ye him, and judge him accord'ing to your law. The Jews therefore said unto him, It is not lawful for us to put any man to death:

32 That the saying of Jesus might be fulfilled', which he spake, signifying what death he should die.

33 Then Pilate entered into the judgment hall again', and called Jesus, and said unto him, Art thou the King of the Jews?

34 Jesus answered him, Sayest thou this thing of thyself', or did others tell it thee of me?

35 Pilate answered, Am I a Jew? Thine own nation and the chief priests have deliv'ered thee unto me: what hast thou done?

36 Jesus answered, My kingdom is not of this world: if my kingdom were of this world, then would my servants fight, that I should not be deliv'ered to the Jews: but now is my kingdom not from hence.

37 Pilate therefore said unto him, Art thou a king then? Jesus answered, Thou sayest that I am a king. To this end was I born, and for this cause came I into the world, that I should bear witness unto the truth. Every one that is of the truth heareth my voice.

38 Pilate saith unto him, What is truth? And when he had said this, he went out again' unto the Jews, and saith unto them, I find in him no fault at all.

39 But ye have a custom, that I should release' unto you one at the passover: will ye therefore that I release' unto you the King of the Jews?

40 Then cried they all again', saying, Not this man, but Barab'bas. Now Barab'bas was a robber.

CHAPTER XIX.

1 Then Pilate therefore took Jesus, and scourged him.

2 And the soldiers platted a crown of thorns, and put it on his head, and they put on him a purple robe,

3 And said, Hail, King of the Jews! and they smote him with their hands.

4 Pilate therefore went forth again', and saith unto them, Behold', I bring him forth to you, that ye may know that I find no fault in him.

5 Then came Jesus forth, wearing the crown of thorns, and the purple robe. And Pilate saith unto them, Behold' the man!

6 When the chief priests therefore and officers saw him, they cried out, saying, Crucify him, crucify him. Pilate saith unto them, Take ye him, and crucify him: for I find no fault in him.

7 The Jews answered him, We have a law, and by our law he ought to die, because' he made himself' the Son of God.

8 ¶ When Pilate therefore heard that saying, he was the more afraid';

9 And went again' into the judgment hall, and saith unto Jesus, Whence art thou? But Jesus gave him no answer.

10 Then saith Pilate unto him, Speakest thou not unto me? knowest thou not that I have power to crucify thee, and have power to release' thee?

11 Jesus answered, Thou couldest have no power at all against' me, except' it were given thee from above': therefore he that deliv'ered me unto thee hath the greater sin.

12 And from thenceforth' Pilate sought to release' him: but the Jews cried out, saying, If thou let this man go, thou art not Cesar's friend: whosoev'er maketh himself' a king speaketh against' Cesar.

13 ¶ When Pilate therefore heard that saying, he brought Jesus forth, and sat down in the judgment seat in a place that is called the Pavement, but in the Hebrew, Gabbatha.

14 And it was the prepara'tion of the passover, and about' the sixth hour: and he saith unto the Jews, Behold' your King!

15 But they cried out, Away' with him, away' with him, crucify him. Pilate saith unto them, Shall I crucify your King? The chief

priests answered, We have no king but Cesar.

16 Then deliv'ered he him therefore unto them to be crucified. And they took Jesus, and led -him away'.

17 And he bearing his cross went forth into a place called the place of a skull, which is called in the Hebrew Golgotha:

18 Where they crucified him, and two others with him, on either side one, and Jesus in the midst.

19 ¶ And Pilate wrote a title, and put it on the cross. And the writing was, JESUS OF NAZARETH THE KING OF THE JEWS.

20 This title then read many of the Jews; for the place where Jesus was crucified was nigh to the city: and it was written in Hebrew, and Greek, and Latin.

21 Then said the chief priests of the Jews to Pilate, Write not, The King of the Jews; but that he said, I am King of the Jews.

22 Pilate answered, What I have written I have written.

23 ¶ Then the soldiers, when they had crucified Jesus, took his garments, and made four parts, to every soldier a part; and also his coat: now the coat was without' seam, woven from the top throughout'.

24 They said therefore among' themselves', Let us not rend it, but cast lots for it, whose it shall be: that the Scripture might be ful-

filled', which saith, They parted my raiment among' them, and for my vesture they did cast lots. These things therefore the soldiers did.

25 ¶ Now there stood by the cross of Jesus his mother, and his mother's sister, Mary the wife of Cleophas, and Mary Magdale'ne.

26 When Jesus therefore saw his mother, and the disci'ple standing by, whom he loved, he saith unto his mother, Woman, behold' thy son!

27 Then saith he to the disci'ple, Behold' thy mother! And from that hour that disci'ple took her unto his own home.

28 ¶ After this,. Jesus knowing that all things were now accom'plished, that the Scripture might be fulfilled', saith, I thirst.

29 Now there was set a vessel full of vinegar: and they filled a spunge with vinegar, and put it upon' hyssop, and put it to his mouth.

30 When Jesus therefore had received' the vinegar, he said, It is finished: and he bowed his head, and gave up the ghost.

31 The Jews therefore, because' it was the prepara'tion, that the bodies should not remain' upon the cross on the sabbath day, (for that sabbath day was a high day,) besought' Pilate that their legs might be broken, and that they might be taken away'.

32 Then came the soldiers, and brake the legs

of the first, and of the other which was crucified with him.

33 But when they came to Jesus, and saw that he was dead alread'y, they brake not his legs:

34 But one of the soldiers with a spear pierced his side, and forthwith' came there out blood and water.

35 And he that saw it bare record, and his record is true; and he knoweth that he saith true, that ye might believe'.

36 For these things were done, that the Scripture should be fulfilled', A bone of him shall not be broken.

37 And again' anoth'er Scripture saith, They shall look on him whom they pierced.

38 ¶ And after this Joseph of Ar'imathe'a, being a disci'ple of Jesus, but secretly for fear of the Jews, besought' Pilate that he might take away' the body of Jesus: and Pilate gave him leave. He came therefore, and took the body of Jesus.

39 And there came also Nicode'mus, (which at the first came to Jesus by night,) and brought a mixture of myrrh and aloes, about' a hundred pound waight.

40 Then took they the body of Jesus, and wound it in linen clothes with the spices, as the manner of the Jews is to bury.

41 Now in the place where he was crucified there was a garden; and in the garden

a new sepulcher, wherein' was never man yet laid.

42 There laid they Jesus therefore because' of the Jews' prepara'tion day; for the sepulcher was nigh at hand.

CHAPTER XX.

1 The first day of the week cometh Mary Magdale'ne early, when it was yet dark, unto the sepulcher, and seeth the stone taken away' from the sepulcher.

2 Then she runneth, and cometh to Simon Peter, and to the other disci'ple, whom Jesus loved, and saith unto them, They have taken away' the Lord out of the sepulcher, and we know not where they have laid him.

•3 Peter therefore went forth, and that other disci'ple, and came to the sepulcher.

4 So they ran both togeth'er: and the other disci'ple did outrun' Peter, and came first to the sepulcher.

5 And he stooping down, and looking in, saw the linen clothes lying; yet went he not in.

6 Then cometh Simon Peter following him, and went into the sepulcher, and seeth the linen clothes lie,

7 And the napkin, that was about' his head, not lying with the linen clothes, but wrapped togeth'er in a place by itself'.

8 Then went in also that other disci'ple,

which came first to the sepulcher, and he saw, and believed'.

9 For as yet they knew not the Scripture, that he must rise again' from the dead.

10 Then the disci'ples went away' again' unto their own home.

11 ¶ But Mary stood without' at the sepulcher weeping: and as she wept, she stooped down, and looked into the sepulcher,

12 And seeth two angels in white sitting, the one at the head, and the other at the feet, where the body of Jesus had lain.

13 And they say unto her, Woman, why weepest thou? She saith unto them, Because' they have taken away' my Lord, and I know not where they have laid him.

14 And when she had thus said, she turned herself' back, and saw Jesus standing, and, knew not that it was Jesus.

15 Jesus saith unto her, Woman, why weepest thou? whom seekest thou? She, suppos'ing him to be the gardener, saith unto him, Sir, if thou have borne him hence, tell me where thou hast laid him, and I will take him away'.

16 Jesus saith unto her, Mary. She turned herself'', and saith unto him, Rabbo'ni; which is to say, Master.

17 Jesus saith unto her, Touch me not; for I am not yet ascend'ed to my Father: but go to my brethren, and say unto them, I ascend'

unto my Father, and your Father; and to my God, and your God.

18 Mary Magdale'ne came and told the disci'- ples that she had seen the Lord, and that he had spoken these things unto her.

19 ¶ Then the same day at evening, being the first day of the week, when the doors were shut whare the disci'ples were assem'bled for fear of the Jews, came Jesus and stood in the midst, and saith unto them, Peace be unto you.

20 And when he had so said, he shewed un- to them his hands and his side. Then were the disci'ples glad, when they saw the Lord.

21 Then said Jesus to them again', Peace be unto you: as my Father hath sent me, even so send I you.

22 And when he had said this, he breathed on them, and saith unto them, Receive' ye the Holy Ghost:

23 Whosesoev'er sins ye remit', thay are re- mit'ted unto them; and whosesoev'er sins ye retain', thay are retained'.

24 ¶ But Thomas, one of the twelve, called Didymus, was not with them when Jesus came.

25 The other disci'ples therefore said unto him, We have seen the Lord. But he said unto them, Except' I shall see in his hands the print of the nails, and put my finger into the print of the nails, and thrust my hand into his side, I will not believe'.

26 ¶ And after eight days again' his disci'-

ples were within', and Thomas with them: then came Jesus, the doors being shut, and stood in the midst, and said, Peace be unto you.

27 Then saith he to Thomas, Reach hither thy finger, and behold' my hands; and reach hither thy hand, and thrust it into my side; and be not faithless, but believ'ing.

28 And Thomas answered and said unto him, My Lord and my God.

29 Jesus saith unto him, Thomas, because' thou hast seen me, thou hast believed': blessed are they that have not seen, and yet have believed'.

30 ¶ And many other signs truly did Jesus in the presence of his disci'ples, which are not written in this book:

31 But these are written, that ye might believe' that Jesus is the Christ, the Son of God; and that believ'ing ye might have life through his name.

CHAPTER XXI.

1 After these things Jesus shewed himself' again' to the disci'ples at the sea of Tibe'rias; and on this wise shewed he himself'.

2 There were togeth'er Simon Peter, and Thomas called Didymus, and Nathan'ael of Cana in Galilee, and the sons of Zebedee, and two other of his disci'ples.

3 Simon Peter saith unto them, I go a fishing. They say unto him, We also go with

thee. They went forth, and entered into a ship imme'diately; and that night they caught nothing.

4 But when the morning was now come, Jesus stood on the shore; but the disci'ples knew not that it was Jesus.

5 Then Jesus saith unto them, Children, have ye any meat? They answered him, No.

6 And he said unto them, Cast the net on the right side of the ship, and ye shall find. They cast therefore, and now they were not able to draw it for the multitude of fishes.

7 Therefore that disci'ple whom Jesus loved saith unto Peter, It is the Lord. Now when Simon Peter heard that it was the Lord, he girt his fisher's coat unto him, (for he was naked,) and did cast himself' into the sea.

8 And the other disci'ples came in a little ship, (for they were not far from land, but as it were two hundred cubits,) dragging the net with fishes.

9 As soon then as they were come to land, they saw a fire of coals there, and fish laid thereon', and bread.

10 Jesus saith unto them, Bring of the fish which ye have now caught.

11 Simon Peter went up, and drew the net to land full of great fishes, a hundred and fifty and three: and for all there were so many, yet was not the net broken.

12 Jesus saith unto them, Come and dine.

And none of the disci'ples durst ask him, Who art thou? knowing that it was the Lord.

13 Jesus then cometh, and taketh bread, and giveth them, and fish likewise.

14 This is now the third time that Jesus shewed himself' to his disci'ples, after that he was risen from the dead.

15 ¶ So when they had dined, Jesus saith to Simon Peter, Simon, son of Jonas, lovest thou me more than these? He saith unto him, Yea, Lord; thou knowest that I love thee. He saith unto him, Feed my lambs.

16 He saith to him again' the second time, Simon, son of Jonas, lovest thou me? He saith unto him, Yea, Lord; thou knowest that I love thee. He saith unto him, Feed my sheep.

17 He saith unto him the third time, Simon, son of Jonas, lovest thou me?· Peter was grieved because' he said unto him the third time, Lovest thou me? And he said unto him, Lord, thou knowest all things; thou knowest that I love thee. Jesus saith unto him, Feed my sheep.

18 Verily, verily, I say unto thee, When thou wast young, thou girdedst thyself', and walkedst whither thou wouldest: but when thou shalt be old, thou shalt stretch forth thy hands, and anoth'er shall gird thee, and carry thee whither thou wouldest not.

19 This spake he, signifying by what death

he should glorify God. And when he had spoken this, he saith unto him, Follow me.

20 Then Peter, turning about', seeth the disci'ple whom Jesus loved following; which also leaned on his breast at supper', and said, Lord, which is he that betray'eth thee?

21 Peter seeing him saith to Jesus, Lord, and what shall this man do?

22 Jesus saith unto him, If I will that he tarry till I come, what is that to thee? follow thou me.

23 Then went this saying abroad' among' the brethren, that that disci'ple should not die: yet Jesus said not unto him, He shall not die; but, If I will that he tarry till I come, what is that to thee?

24 This is the disci'ple which testifieth of these things, and wrote these things: and we know that his testimony is true.

25 And there are also many other things which Jesus did, the which, if they should be written every one, I suppose' that even the world itself' could not contain' the books that should be written. Amen.

THE END.